Raspberry Pi:

The No-Nonsense

Guide

Learn How To Program Your Raspberry Pi 3 Within 12 Hours!

CYBERPUNK UNIVERSITY

Disclaimer Notice:

Table of Contents

Introduction

You saw the cool project Raspberry Pi owners share online; read an article or two about how there is a $35 card-sized computer that you can program to do magical things; You probably even discovered that you always wished you could learn Python programming language; All these conspired to convince you to buy the Raspberry Pi. Now you have it, what's next?

Buying this guide is the best decision you have made as a first-time Raspberry Pi owner. This is a simplified guide that introduces the basics about the Pi including how to connect and configure it, how to write computer programs for it used on-board tools just by drag-and-drop, and how to write your first Python code that controls a blinking LED.

Yes, this is an introductory guide to Raspberry Pi 3, but it goes in a lot deeper than just tell you what it is. With simple step-by-step instructions you will find easy to follow, this book is the best resource to understand how to make your Pi solve your problems. Isn't that why we have computers in the first place?

This eBook is structured into 12 practical chapters that take roughly an hour to do. We have designed the content of the book to be easy to follow for both complete beginners to programming and those with knowledge of other programming languages as well as beginners to Linux and Linux gurus.

Cyberpunk University is committed to producing content that helps learners discover their coding skills and to learn processes that make it easy for them to think of solutions to daily human problems. Many other programming and DIY books are coming in the future so be sure to check our catalog and get the chance to learn even more ways to write programs in different languages that computers can understand.

Find out more about our other books in the series:

1. Python: The No-Nonsense Guide, Learn Python Programming Within 12 Hours!

2. Hacking: The No-Nonsense Guide, Learn Ethical Hacking Within 12 Hours!

Hour 1: Getting Started with the Raspberry Pi

1.1 About Raspberry Foundation

The Raspberry Pi Foundation is a non-profit organization that came up with the ingenious idea to make a full computer the size of a credit card, originally intended for learners in the developing world. The organization released the third edition of its bestselling device in 2015 aptly dubbed Raspberry Pi 3. The tiny machine with a load of capabilities is described as a full desktop PC that can be programmed to do almost anything from creating home servers and media centers to controlling game consoles and document processing.

The Raspberry Pi 3 or simply Pi3 features a 64-bit 1.2 GHz quad-core ARM Cortex A53 processor and comes with Wi-Fi, Bluetooth, Ethernet, and USB on board. Enthusiasts all over the world are constantly posting details of the amazing things they have managed to turn the Pi into, including responsive mirrors, tor routers, video surveillance centers, and even virtual computers for windows operating systems.

Now that you are introduced to Raspberry Pi 3 and possibly already have one on your experimentation bench, you are on the verge of doing amazing things with it using just simple code. You do not need to be a programmer to create dazzling projects with the Pi, but you must be willing and open to learn and try new things.

There is a lot to discover in the Raspberry Pi. If you have already ordered one, then you are in the right path to learning and putting into practice a world of applications of such a tiny yet powerful computer.

In this first hour of discovering the 12 hour guide for programming the Raspberry Pi, we will delve into what it is, a bit of its history, and anything else important you need to know about this compact system.

1.2 What is Raspberry Pi?

The Raspberry Pi Foundation was founded in 2012 to make computers and computer programming instructions accessible to everyone for cheap. While the original mission of the organization was to develop inexpensive computers ready for programming and avail them to students, a much diverse audience has embraced the Pi.

Professional programmers, tinkers, DIYers, and curious hobbyist have embraced the tiny machine and as a result, the support community for the device has grown tremendously around the world in just over five years.

The original Raspberry Pi (called Pi 1 model A) had a SoC (System on Chip) setup built around the tiny but powerful Broadcom BCM 2835 processor commonly used in cellphones. The system included a processor, GPU, and audio and video processing among other features on the low-power chip.

The latest installment, the Pi 3, is even more powerful with greater capabilities including Bluetooth 4.0, Wi-Fi, and a quad-core processing within the same board size as Pi 1. The Pi 3 is a versatile computer that can run many distributions of Linux (including those with desktop environments). However, there are stripped down versions of the open source operating system built specifically for it as you will discover in a bit.

1.3 Technical specs of the Raspberry Pi board

If you are a hardware aficionado, you will be impressed by how much power the credit card-sized Pi computer packs. In the early years of the Pi foundation, two versions of the Raspberry Pi were released. Model A that cost $25 and Model B that cost $35. Model A had no Ethernet port, one less USB port, and half the RAM of its brother Model B.

As the Pi gained more attention and publicity, it was able to pump up the hardware specs significantly while maintaining the price of the Model B, which they decided to focus on. There was only one version of Raspberry Pi 2 and now 3.

So, what exactly do you get when you fork out $35 for Raspberry Pi 3? This:

Raspberry Pi 3 board.

✧ GHz ARM System on Chip (SOC) processor with integrated 1 GB RAM.
✧ 1 HDMI port for digital video and audio output.
✧ 3.5 mm for composite video and analogue output.
✧ 4 USB 2.0 ports.
✧ 1 microSD memory card reader.
✧ 1 Ethernet LAN port.
✧ 1 integrated Wi-Fi and Bluetooth radio antenna.
✧ 1 MicroUSB power port.
✧ GPIO (General Purpose Input/Output) interface.

1.4 Defining the GPIO

The General Purpose Input and Output interface is a set of 40 vertical exposed pins on the Raspberry Pi that are not linked to any specific native functions on the board. These pins are put in place so that the end user can have a low-level access directly to the hardware. He can attach other hardware boards, LCD and LED screens, peripheral devices, and many other kinds of hardware.

As you learn how to program the Pi, you will discover just how ingenious it is that the designers chose to include such an authentic interface for the hardware you will be attaching your own and third party hardware.

1.5 For what do you need this book?

When you order the Raspberry Pi 3, you will get just the bare board -- no case, cables, or power connectors and no guide. Just the board. This means you will have to purchase all the connectors and accessories you will need separately and rely on people like us to learn how to build stuff. Here is a list of the most important things you will need to get (if you don't already have them lying around your workshop).

1. This simplified guide book

2. A stable power source

The Raspberry Pi gets its power via a microUSB port. This means you will need a standard AC to microUSB adapter that can provide consistent 5v power output at a minimum 700mA.

2. A 4GB microSD memory card

The Raspberry Pi foundation recommends that you have a microSD card with at least 4GB available space to install the operating system and applications on the Pi. However, an 8GB or larger card would be ideal. Memory cards are very cheap today, you should consider getting at least a

16GB Class 10 microSD card or larger so that you will never have to worry about storage space.

3. Audio/Visual cables:

What video output do you intend to connect your Pi? If you have a HDTV or one of those newer computer monitors or TVs with HDMI support, you should buy an HDMI cable for digital video and audio output. If your have a standard computer monitor without HDMI support, you will need an HDMI to DVi converter cable for video and a 3.5mm cable for analog audio.

For connection to older TVs, you can buy an RCA cable for video and the 3.5mm stereo cable for audio. If you are unsure which cable is which, head on to the Raspberry Pi website and read official recommendations before you purchase one.

HDMI connector   HDMI to DVI lead   RCA composite video connector

4. Ethernet cable and Router

Although it is not an absolute necessity, connecting the Pi to a network is important, especially for downloading and updating software. It makes everything so easy and fast. An Ethernet cable that connects to a router is necessary if your project relies on you being connected to the internet via LAN.

The Pi comes with an Ethernet port on board, so you will just need to get a cable to plug it to the router. If you would rather use Wi-Fi, the Pi also has that built-in.

5. Mouse and Keyboard:

No matter what you intend to use your Pi for, you will still need a mouse and keyboard to set it up and get it running. Any standard USB keyboard and mouse should work without a problem. These input devices will draw power from the board's USB ports, but a negligible 100mAh or so each. You can check out eLinux.org for a list of verified peripherals compatible with the Raspberry Pi.

Optional: A case:

The Raspberry Pi ships naked. You will get a naked board. For a very small price, though, you can buy a proper case and enclose it to give it a more 'computer' feel and to protect it from the elements and accidental damage. An acrylic or plastic case costs less than $10 but you can also build your own case. Before you purchase one, be sure that you are buying a case for the right Pi because cases for older models will not fit the Pi 3 snugly.

Different Raspberry Pi 3 casings

NOTE: Raspberry Pi Foundation, as I have mentioned earlier, is a non-profit organization. This is why they can afford to sell us such a great computer at a ridiculously low price. The organization runs on support from people like us – through donations and lately by selling official casings of the Raspberry Pi. If you are considering buying a case for your hardware, you should buy one from the foundation and not third-party manufacturers and offer your support a worthy cause.

Hour 2: Setting Up the Raspberry Pi

The Raspberry Pi does not come with an operating system, you have to download and set it up yourself. This, however, is not a weakness but a feature. It means you get to choose from a wide variety of operating systems available to find one that meets your needs.

NOOBS, acronym for New Out Of the Box Software is a program that manages and installs the operating system on your device. This will make it easy for you to install the OS of your choice and to set up the Raspberry Pi.

2.1 Raspbian OS for your Raspberry Pi

There is a wide range of operating systems to choose from for the Pi, all of which are available online for download. Some of the most popular operating systems out there today are Raspbian (Linux distro specially built for the Pi), XBMC, OSMC, RISC OS, OpenELEC, ArchLinux, and Windows IoT Core among others. We have introduced a few of these in Hour 12 of the book.

Raspbian is by far the best and all-round operating system for the Pi. It is also considered the "official" system that every beginner should start with. It is a version of Linux modified for for the Pi and it is what we will be setting up and running in this book. It is packed with all the essential software you need for almost every basic computer task including document processing, browsing the web, checking your emails, and even programming in Python.

If you are new to Linux, you may find Raspbian a bit confusing but do not worry; there are great resources online that will help you navigate this new ocean and explore endless possibilities. A great place to start is the Official Raspberry Pi Beginners Wiki on eLinux.org. They also have a great YouTube channel that explains everything you will need to know to become a master-Raspbian.

2.2 Downloading and Installing Raspbian OS

NOOBS is a great way to test out your new OS and get to know the workings of Raspberry Pi. It makes the OS easy to install right on the memory card. If you would rather not handle the technical aspects of writing an image file to disk, you can grab a pre-installed memory card from Adafruit for about $12. You will find a full guide video on how to work with NOOBS on the Raspberry Pi help page.

Step 1: Get everything ready

NOOBS streamlines the installation process for your Raspbian OS. Get everything you need ready by first downloading NOOBS from this RaspberryPi.org. There are two versions of the download: A larger file for offline and network install, which comes with Raspbian OS in it and a smaller file for online install. I suggest that you download the offline installer and save it on your computer.

You will also need an application to format your SD memory card before you transfer the software on to it. For this, you can download the SD Formatter app from the SD Association. There is a version for both Windows and Mac OS X. Use this tool to format your memory card and prepare it for copying files.

Step 2: Write Image to disk

Once your SD card formatting is complete, extract the zipped files to a folder then transfer all files on to the root of the memory card. These files will include NOOBS and Raspbian OS files.

Wait for the process to complete then eject the memory card.

Step 3: Assemble the Raspberry Pi

Connecting peripheral devices to your Raspberry Pi may be the easiest thing you can do at this stage, but it is important to know what order to follow so that it can recognize all the devices when it boots up.

First, connect the HDMI or monitor cable then connect the USB mouse and keyboard. If you intend to connect the Pi to a LAN network via a router, connect the Ethernet cable next. Finally, insert the memory card with your copied NOOBS and Raspbian OS files.

Because Raspberry Pi does not have a power switch, it powers on the moment you connect and turn on the power. Connect the power USB cable last then switch power on. Your newest computer will boot to the NOOBS screen which will allow you to set up the OS.

Step 4: Install Raspbian OS

The NOOBS system will take a couple of minutes to get all the devices ready. Let it do its thing, eventually it will complete the checks and take you to a screen prompting you to install an operating system.

At the bottom of this screen, you will see the options to choose your language and keyboard layout. Make your selections then click the check box next to the Raspbian option and click install to initiate the process.

That is it! NOOBS will take over and run the installation process, which could take anywhere between ten and twenty minutes. When the setup is complete, NOOBS will restart the Pi and it will boot right to the new Linux Raspbian OS desktop where you can begin configuring everything else.

Note: Should the installation process require a username and password, the defaults to use are:

>**Username**: pi

>**Password**: raspberry

Step 5: Configure Wi-Fi or LAN network

The Raspbian OS has a very intuitive screen featuring a 'start' Pi menu where you can start applications and tools, open the file browser or go online— pretty much everything you would expect on a full-fledged desktop environment. First though, you should set up a network connection.

To connect to a Wi-Fi network, click on the network icon on the top right corner. It is the icon with two computers.

Select your Wi-Fi network by clicking on its SSID. This will prompt you to enter a password. Enter the wireless network password then click OK to connect.

The process is the same when you are connecting to Ethernet wired network.

Step 6: Connect Bluetooth Devices

If you have Bluetooth devices such as a keyboard and mouse or speakers, you will need to pair them with the Raspberry Pi before you can use them. This, however, depends on the devices and your pairing preferences.

The process is pretty straightforward on Raspbian. Simply click the Bluetooth icon on the top right corner of the screen and select 'Add Device'. The system will scan for discoverable Bluetooth devices and when it finds the device you want to pair, simply click on it and click pair. A simplified pairing process will guide you on what to do until the process is completed.

That is it as far as setting up and configuring your Pi goes! As you can see, the process has been simplified by NOOBS. Setting up Raspberry Pi 1 and 2 was such a pain, but thanks to the NOOBS program, anyone can now get the Pi running without writing cryptic lines of code. If anything should go wrong during the setup process, just start over more carefully and follow the above process to re-install Raspbian.

Hour 3: Installing Raspbian OS the Hard Way

Installing an operating system on a Raspberry Pi is too easy with NOOBS, which makes sense because that is what NOOBS was developed for. Unfortunately, the process explained in the last hour does not go deep to show exactly what is happening during the installation process. If you are the kind of person who likes to do things the hard way, in this hour that is exactly what we are going to focus on.

3.1 Is the hard way the better way?

One of the biggest problem that beginners face when trying to install Raspbian or any other OS for that matter on Raspberry Pi is low space. If you have a 4GB microSD card, you will fit the NOOBS files on it, but there may not be sufficient space to carry out the installation because it involves expanding files, not to mention space for your files after the installation is complete.

Besides, if you have gone as far as buy your own Pi, it would be understandable that you want to use the more technical approach to installing the OS. As you begin programming the Pi, it will pay off having a clear understanding of how the system works and how to set it up without taking shortcuts.

Also, considering that this book does not dive deep into the various ways to test an OS before installing it on your Pi, it will be important to know how to perform the setup process using the terminal for when you install another operating system or to repair the current one.

In this hour, we will look at how to install Raspbian OS on your Pi using the not-too-easy approach. Let's start.

Step 1: Get everything ready

Head over to the Raspberry Pi Downloads page and download the latest Raspbian OS image. There are two versions of the Raspbian OS image: a pixel image Raspbian Jessie, and the Raspbian Jessie Lite, a minimal version of the OS that is smaller in size. Decide which one you wish to install then download it.

You will also need a tool to extract the file image from the archive. You can use 7Zip for windows or Unarchiver for Mac. Both these tools are available free online.

As with the previous method, you will need a tool to format your memory card. Use the SD Formatter from SDcard.org you downloaded in the previous hour. Finally, you will need a tool to write the downloaded OS files you extract from the archive on to the memory card. You can download the Win32 Disk Imager for that. You can download it from Sourceforge.

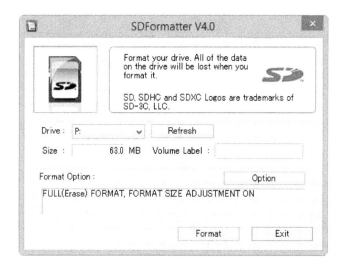

MicroSD Formatting app SDFormatter

Step 2: Writing image to disk

Begin the installation by formatting the disk. You can begin the process and let it run in the background. Meanwhile, extract the .img file of the OS image in the archive you downloaded and place it on a folder where you can easily access.

Run the Win32 Disk Imager with administrative rights on Windows. Select the Raspbian OS .img file you extracted and load it. When the SD card formatting is complete, select the disk address as the destination on the Win32 Disk Imager then click Write to begin the process.

Writing to the disk may take up to 30 minutes. Be patient till it is done then remove the SD card.

Step 3: Installing Raspbian OS on the Pi

This is the step where the excitement begins. As explained in the previous hour, the order in which you connect your devices to the Pi matters. It is recommended that you do not power on the device before you connect the keyboard and mouse.

Insert the memory card and plug in the mouse and keyboard then connect the power cable. The Pi should power on and start booting after you turn the power on.

If you are prompted to enter your credentials the defaults are:

Login: pi

Password: raspberry

When boot up is complete, you will be taken to the configuration screen titled 'Setup Options'. This is how it should look like:

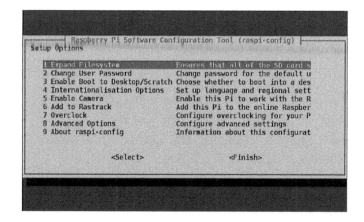

If you do not see the setup options screen you can get to it by starting the terminal then entering the following command:

 sudo raspi-config

Select the first option:

 1 Expand Filesystem

Do this by pressing the return key on the keyboard (Enter). Setup will use up all the space in the SD card as a single partition to install the operating system. It does this by expanding the Raspian OS image to fit the available storage space.

When this is done, you will return to the same screen where you can then select the third option:

 3 Enable Boot to Desktop/Scratch

In the next screen, you will be asked to 'Choose boot option'. Select the second option:

 Desktop Log in as user 'pi' at the graphical desktop

Click OK or press enter. We select this option so that when the Raspbian boots up, each time it will take us to the graphical user interface desktop and not the Terminal.

When this is done, the raspi-config will take you back to the previous window, the Setup Options page.

Step 4: Reboot

In some cases, the Pi may automatically reboot after the setup is done. If it does not, you may have to boot it manually. You can do this on the Terminal using the command:

sudo reboot

If everything went right during the setup, the Pi should boot to a beautiful graphical user interface desktop. You are now ready to start doing magic with your Pi.

Raspbian OS desktop on Raspberry Pi 3

3.6 Understanding the raspi-config window

The Raspberry Pi configuration window, powered by raspi-config engine, has more options than we used in the setup process above. As you begin to understand how your device works, it is good for you to know what each of the nine items on the Setup Options window does for when you will need to use it. All of them have a brief explanation about what they do to their right but here is a summary that may be easier to understand:

1. Expand Filesystem: As mentioned, this option expands the operating system image to occupy the entire disk. You do not need to expand the image but it is highly recommended that you do so to make use of all the storage space available.

Any unused space on the SD card may not be recognized by the Pi, which means it will go to waste and you will have lesser disk space for your projects.

2. Change User Password: This is pretty straightforward. You can choose change the default password from raspberry on this screen.

3. Enable Boot to Desktop/Scratch: This option allows you to change where your Pi boots to. You can choose to boot straight to Scratch, to the Terminal, or to the gui desktop.

4. Internationalisation Options: Here you can set or change your locale, timezone, and keyboard layout. Note that you will need to reboot the Pi to apply your changes.

5. Enable Camera: Enable this to use the Raspberry Pi Camera Module. When enabled, the system will dedicate at least 128MB of RAM to the GPU.

6. Add to Rastrack: This is a handy feature if you want to know who else around you uses the Pi. It is user-contributed and runs on Google's Maps to allow users to add their locations. Rastrack shows a heat map of where Pi users are around the world.

7. Overclock: The default clock speed of the Pi's processor is 700MHz but you can pump it up to 1000MHz with this option. Note that the results you achieve may vary and that overclocking too high could cause instability that reduces the life of your Pi.

8. Advanced options: There are several important options under this item, some of which we will look at in the next steps we will cover in the book. They are:

Overscan	Hostname	Memory Split	SSH	Device tree
SPI	I2C	Serial	Audio	Update

9. About raspi-config: A two-sentence summary of what the Pi is all about.

Hour 4: The Basics about Raspbian OS

Learning how to work with and program your Raspberry Pi is much easier and faster when you start somewhere familiar. Where could be better than a dynamic graphical user interface of Raspbian OS?

Raspbian was developed with a goal to become the top OS of choice for all kinds of Pi users – from beginners like you to the veterans who pride themselves in having owned the very first Raspberry Pi model A back in 2012.

Raspbian was developed based on the Debian distribution of Linux, hence the reason they are very similar in many ways. Debian has millions of users around the world who have contributed a massive knowledge base and documentation published on the web. Raspbian users can tap on this wealth of information to learn broadly and deeply about Raspbian OS. Almost every piece of information about Debian OS you find on the web also applies to Raspbian OS of the same version on the Pi.

4.1 Connecting to a network

One of the very first things that Pi users do as soon as they have set up their devices is to connect to the internet – either by setting up the LAN or by connecting to Wi-Fi. The setup process is pretty simple.

If connecting to a router via an Ethernet cable, you need to configure your routers DHCP so that you can easily plug in the cable and connect to it. If you already have a router and a network, we will assume you have already figured out its settings and how to add a new computer to the network.

For Wi-Fi connections, it is even easier to set up the Pi to join the network and connect to the internet. Raspbian comes with a handy Wi-Fi Config tool, whose shortcut is placed on the desktop. All you just need to double-click and follow simple guided steps to connect to the hotspot or Wi-Fi network.

If you have to scan for networks, you can use the following commands on the LXTerminal:

sudo iwlist wlan0 scan

This command will scan and list all the available networks for you to choose the one you want to connect to.

To connect to the network manually, open the nano editor and modify the configuration file wpa-supplicant using the following command:

sudo nano /etc/wpa_supplicant/wpa_supplicant.conf

Scroll to the bottom of the file and enter the network information in this format:

network = {

ssid = "[Wi-Fi_ESSID]"

psk = "[Wi-Fi_password]"

}

Save the file and the wpa-supplicant will begin to connect to the network in a few seconds.

4.2 Using Raspbian on Raspberry Pi as a desktop PC

The most important part of setting up your Raspberry Pi is installing the operating system. Once you are done with this step, and the OS of your choice is running seamlessly, you can decide to turn your Pi into anything you want – from a desktop PC or server to a bot or a game console.

Since we have installed the most basic (and most suited) operating system on the Pi, we will first look at what you need to do to turn it into a potent PC that you can use for anything that your Windows, Linux, or Mac desktop computer does.

Considering that Raspbian OS is based on Linux kernel, the following steps will be much easier for you if you are familiar with the Linux platform in general. Do not worry though, you will still find it easy to learn if this is your first encounter with the Linux operating system. This guide is written for you.

4.3 Exploring apps and packages

If you have already explored around the desktop of the Raspbian OS, you may have noticed that it comes pre-installed with several tools you would need for a basic PC. As long as your display is good, you can easily navigate to any apps (called packages) or settings installed by double-clicking the icon shortcuts on the desktop and via the 'Start' button on the top left corner of the screen.

Under the office header, you find the entire suite of word processor, spreadsheet, presentation, database, etc. You will also find shortcuts on the desktop to popular tools and packages you will be using including Python IDLE and games.

There is an even easier way to explore hundreds of other packages and download them with ease: the Raspbian store also dubbed The Pi Store. You can add the Pi Store app to your installation using the command:

    sudo apt-get update && sudo apt-get install pistore

4.4 Updating Software

The first thing you should do is upgrade the system's package list.

Open the LXTerminal by double-clicking the shortcut on the desktop or press Ctrl+Alt+T on your keyboard. Then enter this code to update the package list:

    sudo apt-get update

You may be asked to enter root password. The default root username is 'root' and the password is 'root'.

Next, upgrade the packages already installed using the following command:

    sudo apt-get dist-upgrade

This command enables the APT (Advanced Packaging Tool) to update your packages regularly. It will also download and install any new kernel and firmware updates of the Debian package. Note, however, that these packages are not frequently updated; updates are only rolled out after extensive testing.

4.5 Installing new software

There is a very simple way to install software on your Pi than having to go online on a browser, download a package, unzip it, and begin configuration: The APT tool.

This tool allows you to install, update, and uninstall packages with a simple command. If a software program is packaged for Debian and it is developed to work on the Pi's ARM architecture, then you should be able to install it using the apt-get command.

As you have noticed above, you will need to gain root access using the sudo command to use apt-get. The command sudo stands for Super User DO and it essentially grants the installation tool superuser (system-level) privileges to configure the packages. This is the reason you have to enter a password to be logged in as root or a sudoer.

To see a list of software sources that APT keeps, you can open the sources.list file stored in the directory /etc/apt/. You will find out as you get more experience why this is important.

The command to install a package takes this format:

    sudo apt-get install package_name

The update procedure we covered in the previous section updates all the packages including firmware. If you have limited bandwidth or disk space

and wish to update only a specific package at a time, you can use this
command:

sudo apt-get update package_name

Here is the apt command you will use to uninstall a package:

sudo apt-get remove package_name

This will prompt you to confirm the uninstallation with a y/n question.
However, if you do not want to be constantly asked to confirm, you can use
the –y flag after the package_name to auto confirm.

An alternative command to remove a program is purge. The purge APT
command removes the package and all its associated configuration files. The
command looks like this:

sudo apt-get purge package_name

It is advisable that you do not use purge unless you know what you are doing.

If you have the name of a package you wish to install, you can search for it
using the command:

apt-cache search package_name

Finally, the tree command may come in handy, especially if you want to get
even more familiar with the terminal interface. This command visualizes the
structure of your working directory (called present working directory or
pwd). Type the command and see how it works.

tree

Hour 5: Writing a Simple Game with Scratch on Raspberry Pi

Now that we have covered all the basics about the Raspberry Pi, our next step is to learn how to use it to make things happen. In this hour, we are going to learn how to develop a simple game using a bundled tool whose shortcut you will find on the desktop: Scratch.

This hour, you will learn to get around the interface of scratch, practice using blocks to program an object to move, change sprites, and even create your own sprites.

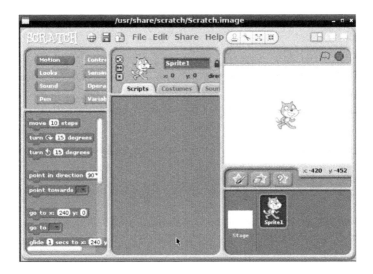

Fig 1: Scratch on Raspberry Pi

5.1 What is scratch?

Scratch is a visual programming tool that comes with the Raspbian OS. It allows you to create games and animations with ease using a drag-and-drop interface. This tool makes programming easy, and fun—even addicting. You can also use an online browser version of this tool.

With scratch, we will be able to create a simple game with guidance on this book, but later you can practice on your own to create interactive stories, animations, and even use it to program the GPIO pins on the Pi. This tool is the best introduction to code and especially game programming because you will not need to write the actual code. It will help you understand the general aspects and techniques of programming that will lay the foundation for your understanding of the more complex procedures later on.

Scratch is already installed on your Pi, you will not need to download or install anything. Simply open the package from the desktop icon and you are good to go. The main window of the app is split into three sections:

1. The tools you will need to create your game are on the left.
2. The middle section is your working area where you will create the sprites and steps.
3. The program you create will run on the right section.

Your game will be made up of sprites (pictures) that follow scripts (steps) you create. The scripts are what we use to control what the program does when a certain condition is met, such as when the player presses a key.

On the top left corner, you will see eight buttons (tools). They are: Motion, Looks, Sound, Pen, Control, Sensing, Operations, and Variables. These are the categories of the pieces we will be dragging and adding on to the scripts to build our game.

Let's get started.

5.2 Variables

Before we can begin creating our game on Scratch, there are a few things we must understand. First, is that the program should able to remember something. Could be a shape, a number, an event, text—anything. We will do this using variables.

A variable is a small allocation of computer memory that a program stores data in. We will create several variables during the game to store game data. If you have learnt other languages of programming, such as Python, you will discover that there are different types of variables, each specific to storing a particular type of data. In this section, however, you do not need to worry about all that.

CyberPunk University has a comprehensive yet simplified eBook that can help you understand full computer programming 'Python: The No-Nonsense Guide'. Sooner or later, if you find programming with the Raspberry Pi fun and productive, you will need a full guide such as this to learn everything.

Every variable we will create will have an assigned value that can be called upon during the running of the program, evaluated, and results output in different ways.

5.3 Blocks

We are going to create several scripts, and they will need to communicate in different ways. In some instances, we will use variables, but we will use messages mostly when programming with Scratch. Blocks of code are used on this platform to trigger scripts just the way the keyboard keys do when pressed. When a script is set to broadcast a message, all the scripts will be triggered to start with 'When I Receive…''

Just like variables, each message will have an assigned name when we create it. It must also be linked to a script which will trigger it to initiate a broadcast.

Now that you know variables and messages, we can begin designing our simple game.

5.4 Creating a simple arcade game based on the popular Ping pong

We are going to create a simple Ping pong game from scratch using Scratch and call it Punk Pong. Sounds catchy, doesn't it?

Ping Pong is an old arcade one or two player video game featuring a ball and two bats. The game is played by preventing the ball from touching the player's goal i.e. beyond the bat. It looks something like this:

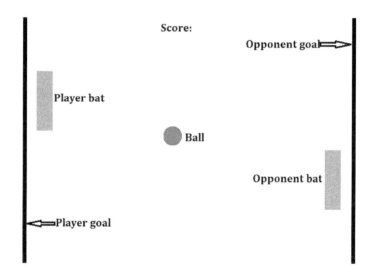

Fig 2: Layout of the Punk pong game we are going to create.

Step 1: Setting up Scratch

The first thing we will do is start a new workspace on scratch. When you open the program window, there will be the cat scratch by default. Right-click it and click 'Delete'.

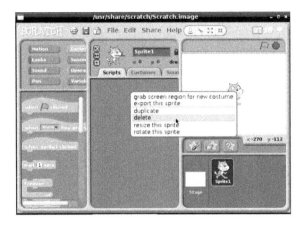

Fig 3: Creating a blank workspace

This will give us a free workspace to begin creating the game.

We are going to create five sprites for this game: The ball, player bat, opponent bat, player goal, and opponent goal.

Click on the 'Create New Sprite' icon and draw the ball. You will first need to select the color, then draw on the canvas and fill the ball with paint of the same color using the bucket tool. To draw a perfect circle and not an oval, press SHIFT on the keyboard while drawing.

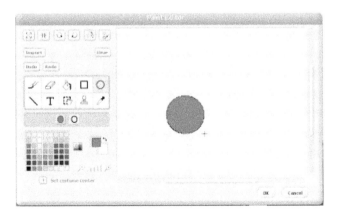

Fig 4: Drawing the ball sprite

When done drawing, click OK then assign the sprite a new name: ball.

Using the same procedure, create the remaining four sprites, making sure to assign them appropriate names:

- playerbat
- opponentbat
- playergoal
- opponentgoal

Once you have created and saved all the objects, you can drag them around the screen and place them in their rightful positions as in Fig 2.

Step 2: Making the ball bouncy

Double-click on the ball sprite. Its scripts section should be blank, but we can make it move around by adding a few instructions.

On the left section of the workspace, click on the orange 'Control' button to reveal associated steps under it.

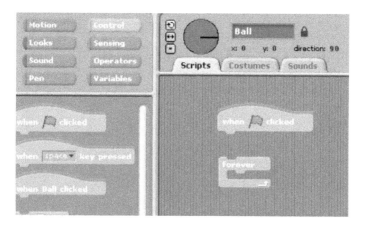

Fig 5: Programming the ball

Add the 'when clicked' piece with a green flag to the ball's logic then drag to position it high on the workspace.

Click on the '**Motion**' button and choose the 'point in direction' code then fit it under the first. Adjust the angle inside the block to 45.

The 'forever' orange loop block should fit after the 'point in direction' code. Click on the '**Motion**' button again and add 'move 10 steps' to fit inside the forever block. Change the steps from 10 to 5. This essentially means that the ball will move 5 steps in a 45 degree direction over and over again when clicked.

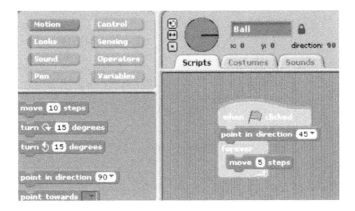

Fig 6: Programming the ball

To ensure that the ball is set to the center of the screen when the game starts, we will add a 'go to' piece defining the position as x and y coordinates. This will reset the ball position when the green start flag is clicked. We will also want the ball to bounce off the edges, we will add more code blocks as shown below:

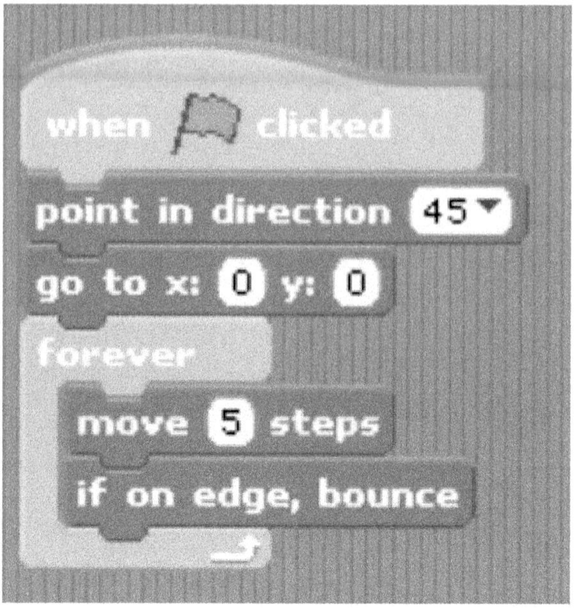

Fig 7: Defining the bat edge and centering the ball

Step 3: The ball and the bat

The players can defend their goals by getting the ball to hit the bat and bounce off it. We are going to program the ball such that when it hits a bat, it bounces off in a random direction.

Drag two orange 'if' blocks and position them after the last instruction within the 'forever' block. You can also alter the direction of the ball by clicking the rotate button to its left. The result should look like this.

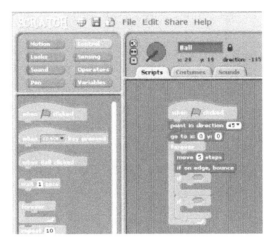

Fig 8: The ball and the bat

The two 'if' blocks will only execute the blocks within them when a condition they test equals true. We will insert conditions from the 'Sensing' button, dragging 'touching' to the 'if' blocks and changing the first to **playerbat** and the second to **opponentbat**.

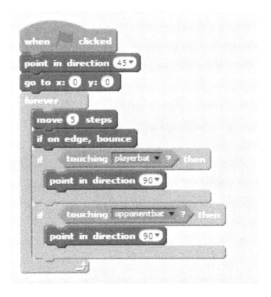

Fig 9: Programming ball bounce

We will also need to insert actions of code to execute when the conditions being tested return true. In this case, we will add point in direction blocks to each of the 'if' statements blocks and find an operator from the '**Operator**' button. We will then randomize the angle between 10 and 170.

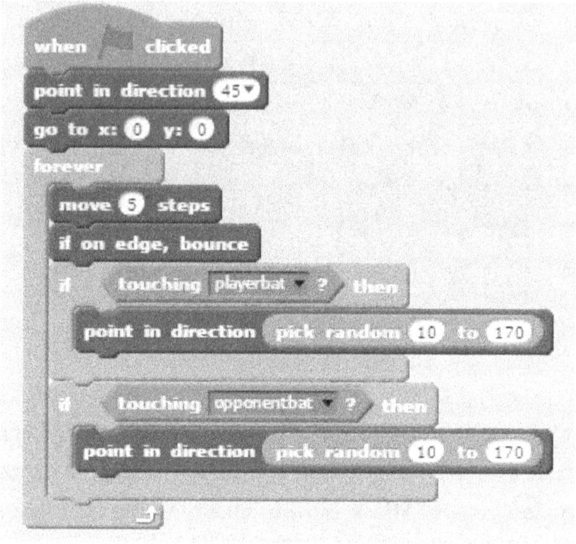

Fig 10: Randomizing the ball bounce

Fit the 'pick random' operator nicely within 'point in direction' block to randomize the direction the ball takes after hitting the playerbat or the opponentbat.

Step 4: Configuring player control

For the game to be playable, the player should be able to control the playerbat. We will program it such that the playerbat can be moved up and down the Y axis using the mouse.

Double click the playerbat sprite and add the objects as shown in the image. The process is pretty much the same as when you programmed the ball.

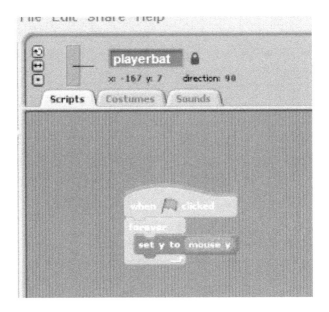

Fig 11: Setting up player input

When the player moves the mouse button up and down, the **playerbat** sprite will move along with it. Click on the green flag to test it out.

Step 5: Program the opponentbat to play intelligently

We are going to make our game playable by automating the opponent. Punk pong will be a single player game where the player plays against the computer. To make an intelligent opponent, we are going to dabble in some Artificial Intelligence.

Artificial intelligence is basically programming the computer to make decisions based on the information it receives. We will want the computer, in this case opponentbat, to prevent the ball from touching the opponent goal. This means that as the ball moves up and down the Y axis, the computer's bat should move along with it.

Double click on the **opponentbat** and blocks as shown in fig 12.

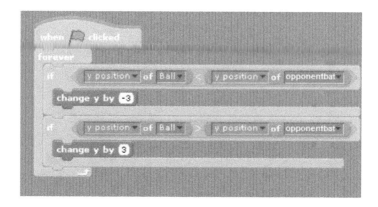

Fig 12: Programming computer opponent player

At this point, your Punk pong game is playable, but it cannot keep scores. We are going to make it even more interesting in the next step.

Step 6: Variables and keeping score

At this stage, we are going to create two new variables for scores: one for the player and another for the opponent.

Click on the red '**Variables**' menu item then click 'Make a variable'. Give it a name such as 'Player Score' then click on the 'For all sprites' radio button and click OK. Do the same for the 'Opponent Score'.

You should notice that a little counter is automatically added to the game screen.

Double click the ball sprite again to bring up its script code. To reset the scores at the beginning of the game, add two new code blocks just below 'when clicked' as shown:

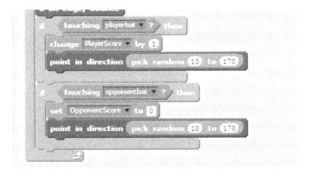

Fig 13: Randomizing ball bounce

The next thing we will do is configure the game such that when the ball hits the goal, the score increases by 1. We are going to add this code within the 'forever' loop. Modify your blocks to look like this:

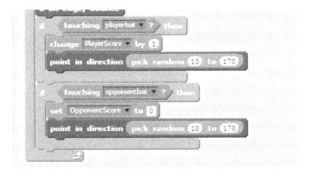

Fig 14: Configuring scores

Finally, we can add conditions to test to end the game if they return positive. In this case, we can set the game score to 5. When the ball touches the player's or opponent's goal five times, the game ends. Add two if conditions within the 'forever' loop and add a condition to test the scores for each as shown.

Fig 15: Programming game end

The 'stop all' block with a red stop sign ends the game.

5.5 Conclusion

Congratulations on completing your first game on Raspberry Pi. You can now test your game, and go back to the editing table to improve the drawings and even tweak other blocks in the script.

In the next hour, we will briefly look at what GPIO is and how it works, then we can figure out how to program Punk pong to output signals through it.

Hour 6: The GPIO (General Purpose Input and Output)

The GPIO pins of the Raspberry Pi are one of the most outstanding features of the board that makes it a favorite platform for budding programmers. These pins are the interface point through which the computer can communicate with other circuits and devices such as extensions boards and custom circuits. We are going to make some pretty cool stuff that make use of these pins.

Before we can get to that point, we first have to know the basics about them.

Warning: Experimenting with the GPIO pins can be very risky. A little short circuiting could brick your Pi, just like that. You should read widely about what to plug in to the pins and how to be careful not to cause damage to your board through proper insulation and care handling.

6.1 Understanding the GPIO on Raspberry Pi

Before you can begin working with the GPIO pins on your Pi, it is vital that you understand what the different types of pins there are, how you can enable the modules, and get to know what a breakout kit is.

Assuming that you own a Raspberry Pi 3, your board should have 40 pins in total, arranged in two rows of 20. Earlier models of the Pi had had 26 pins.

The pinout table below is a layout of the functions of the 40 pins:

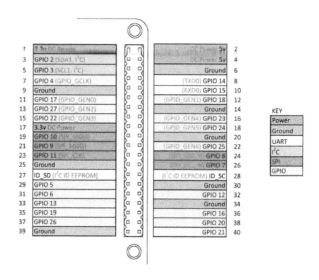

Fig 16: GPIO Pins (Image source: mcmelectronics.com)

As you can see on the color-coded image, there are more than just standard pins on the GPIO. Let us look at what each of the different types of pins refer to.

Power pins: These are pins that pull power directly from the Pi board. There are two types of pins—pin 1 and 17 that draw 3.3v and pin 2 and 4 that draw 5v.

GND: These are pins that are used to ground connected devices. It does not matter which ground pin you connect to, they are all the same.

UART: UART is an acronym for Universal Asynchronous Receiver and transmitter. The UART pins are serial in nature and are used to communicate with devices that support asynchronous interfaces.

I2C: This stands for Inter-Integrated Circuit, hence the square symbol after the I. It is acceptable to refer to it as I2C. These pins are used to connect hardware modules that support the I2C protocol. Typically, a device using this interface will be connected to two pins.

SPI: SPI is an acronym for Serial Peripheral Interface Bus. SPI pins are used to connect devices that support the SPI protocol to enable the Pi to 'talk' to them. It is pretty much similar to I2C except that they use different protocols to communicate.

GPIO: GPIO are the standard pins that are used for simple tasks such as turning devices on and off. We will be connecting our LEDS to these pins.

You do not need to memorize this table, or the definitions of the acronyms. What is important is that you understand what they actually do. With time and experience, you will get to master the purpose of each type of pins as the jargon and abbreviations will begin make more sense.

We recommend that you print out the pin layout chart provided along with this eBook as bonus material and stick it somewhere close to your work bench so that you can refer to it any time you need to.

In the next hour, we will take a step further into the world of programming the Raspberry Pi hardware by extending the capabilities of our Punk pong game.

Hour 7: Making an LED Blink with Scratch GPIO on Raspberry Pi

In the last six hours of learning how get around the hardware and software of your new Raspberry Pi, we have been covering the basics. What we will cover in this hour is also basic, but it is a stride in that it brings together two elements that are seemingly separate yet can seamlessly work together: writing a program that makes a hardware do things.

The whole point of learning to program with the Pi is to make the computer do solve problems by doing things. Otherwise we might just as well use your laptop to learn Linux and Python, or work with the online version of scratch accessible via your browser. You have reason to be very excited this hour because it is an introduction to what you have been looking forward to do with your newest micro-computer.

7.1 Getting everything ready

For the exercises in this hour, you are going to need:

1. Raspberry Pi 3
2. The working Punk pong game we created in Hour 5.
3. A breadboard.
4. 1 LED bulb.
5. 1K Ohm Resistor (Brown, Black, Red)
5. 2 male to female jumper wires.

Note: It is important that you have a clear working space when working on, especially because there is always danger in working with electrical current, no matter how small the voltage. Working in a cluttered environment is a recipe for disaster because even the tiniest strands of wire can cause catastrophic short circuits that could brick your Raspberry Pi or even cause fires.

As you learned in the previous hour in the introduction to the GPIO, the Pi outputs two different voltages that we will use to power the Pi: 3.3 and 5V.

If you took a short while off between the last and this exercise, spare a few minutes to familiarize yourself with the location of the power and grounding pins because that is what we will be using in this exercise.

7.2 Usage and basic capabilities of GPIO server

The version of Scratch for the Raspberry Pi that was released in September 2015, which also comes with the Raspbian Jessie operating system you installed on your Pi, introduces a new GPIO server. This tool is used to drive LEDs, HATS, buzzers and other devices and components. This exercise will serve to introduce the basics of what you can do with the GPIO server but there is a lot more you will discover on your own.

Before you can use the GPIO pins on the Pi, you must first initialize the GPIO server. There are three ways you can do this:

1. From the Edit menu, choose 'Start GPIO server' to turn it on. If the server is already running, the item on the menu will change to 'Stop GPIO server'.
2. Using the gpioserveron broadcast on Scratch. You can then use gpioserveroff to turn it off.
3. Simply save your project with the GPIO server running and the status will be saved. When you initialize your project, the GPIO server will be automatically enabled.

In our case, we are going to use the broadcast method to initialize the inbuilt GPIO server, which we can then program in our Punk pong Scratch game to light up the LED.

Without any further setup, we will be able to access the basics of the GPIO capabilities by simply dragging the broadcast blocks under the orange Control button.

7.3 Connecting the hardware

Before we can write the code that makes the magic happen, we will first prepare the platform: assembling the circuitry.

This book assumes that you have basic knowledge of how to use a breadboard, how to connect wires, and more importantly, how electricity works and why we require male to female jumper cables. If you are not well versed with this part of working with the Pi, we recommend that you take some time to read various online resources to bring you up to speed before you attempt these connections.

Assemble the LED bulb and the resistor in series as shown in the figure below:

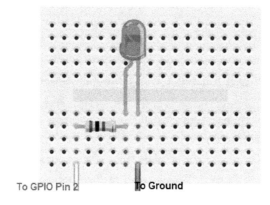

Fig 17: Connecting the circuits

Note that the longer leg of the LED is the positive, which you will connect to pin 2. The shorter leg is the negative, which connects to any ground pin on the Pi. Remember that ground pins are 6, 9, 14, 20, 25, 30, 34, and 39.

Use the female to male jumper wires to connect the breadboard to the GPIO pins on the Raspberry Pi.

When the connections are set, you can now move on to configuring our game to light up the LED.

7.4 Configuring GPIO pins on Scratch

Because we will be configuring the Raspberry Pi to send power to a pin of our choice when a certain condition is met, we must first define that condition. We can configure the game to trigger the LED light to turn on when an even occurs by finding its exact position on the script of the game.

For this exercise, we are going to configure the LED to light up when the player scores.

We are going to create three blocks for this: a broadcast block to turn on the pin when the player scores (we will be use pin 2), a block to delay the on status for the LED by one second, and another to turn it off.

Start your scratch app and load the Punk pong game we created. It should begin exactly where you left it.

We are going to add the two broadcast blocks to the script from the Control menu. Click on the orange Control button on the top left section of the screen then scroll down on the bottom section to find the broadcast block.

Considering that our game executes blocks according to the order they are arranged, we will then need to find the blocks that triggers the player's score. If you remember well, it is the *'change PlayerScore by 1'* variable block within the forever block.

Fig 18: Where to program the GPIO broadcast

When you set a pin to be an output, it is connected to the Scratch sensor variable system. This means that it will appear in the list of possible values you can choose from the sensor blocks as well.

Drag the first broadcast blog and position it between the 'change PlayerScore by 1' variable block and the blue 'go to x: 0 y: 0' block. Next, designate the kind of signal you will send.

Click on the list box within the block to bring up a menu which allows you to enter a new command. Click '*new*' and when the input box appears, enter your new command.

Pins are defined by their numbers on the Raspberry Pi. What we will need to do is define the command in a similar format and the GPIO server will execute it without further configuration from our end. In this case, simply enter the message '*pin2on*' to turn on pin number 2.

Drag a '*wait 1 secs*' block and position it just below the one we just configured to turn on pin 2 on the GPIO.

We are going to leave its value the way it is but if you prefer you can change the duration of wait to 2 or 3 secs. You should not set it higher than that though because it will delay the reset and restart of the game for too long. Remember that Scratch executes the blocks in order, so if you set the wait for 10 secs, the LED will light for 10 seconds before the next block is executed.

Next, drag another broadcast block and position it beneath the '*wait 1 secs*' control block. Click on it to change its value, click new and on the input box, enter '*pin2off*'.

That is pretty much it.

In summation, the three blocks of scripts we added to our game will be triggered when the PlayerScore value increases by 1. The GPIO server will turn on pin 2 on, which will cause the raspberry Pi to supply 5v of power to pin number 2. This state will be maintained for 1 second (or whatever duration you specify on the '*wait 1 secs*' block and after that, power to the pin will be turned off and the game resumed.

You can also test the turn on and turn off broadcast commands by double-clicking the blocks. If they are properly configured, and the breadboard and GPIO pins properly connected, the LED should light right up.

Now, play the Punk pong game and see what happens when you score.

7.5 Conclusion

If your project was as successful as mine, you should be lighting up the LED every time you score in the game you created with Scratch. That was not difficult was it?

Scratch is an easy to understand and even easier to use programming platform that you can use for all kinds of content—not just games. There is also a lot you can make the Raspberry Pi GPIO server do besides light up a LED. Since you have already learnt the basics, you should go back to the beginning of hour 5 and create your own game, art, or storyline, and make it do all kinds of things using the GPIO server including checking the wiring operations of your circuitry.

Since we have done all this without any complex or detailed instructions, imagine what else you can do when you expand your learning environment and spend days, weeks, or even months working on it? The official Scratch website, https://scratch.mit.edu/, is resource-rich and has a vibrant community that has been creating and remixing all kinds of projects since 2012. Head on there to discover what else you can learn.

Hour 8: Introduction to the Shell on Raspberry Pi

When you installed Raspbian OS, one of the first things you discovered is that it has an easy to use graphical user interface similar to what you may be used to in Windows or Mac OS. Getting around the computer, creating and manipulating files, and managing packages is much easier with the interface. You can initialize your web browser by clicking on a link, start Scratch by double-clicking an icon on the desktop, and search for files by opening folder icons.

The thing is, a graphical user interface is not as powerful as a human-computer interaction point can be. This is where the command line interface (CLI) comes in. Because Raspbian OS is based on Linux kernel, its command line interface is known as the Shell or the Terminal.

8.1 What is the Shell or Terminal

The Shell, as we will refer the Raspbian terminal from this point on, is a text-based interface where you enter commands to get a response. If you are a Windows or Mac aficionado and have never encountered a command line interface before, do not worry. It may seem a bit confusing at first but with a bit of guidance and lots of practice, everything will begin to make sense and learning to use it will pay huge dividends in the near future, especially since you have shown interest in computer and machine programming.

To start the Shell on Raspbian, double-click on the LXTerminal program shortcut on the desktop or press Ctrl+Alt+T on your keyboard. The program window should look like Fig 21.

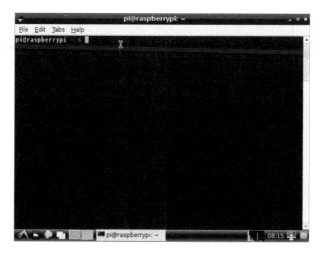

Fig 21: The LXTerminal running on Raspbian OS on the Raspberry Pi 3

8.2 Discovering basic commands in Unix

The line of text pi@raspberrypi ~ $ is the command prompt. This line shows that the system is ready and on stand-by to receive input from you. Enter the following and press enter:

pwd

What you entered is a command, in this case asking the Shell to Print Working Directory. This is simply a way to ask the Shell to show which folder you are currently working on. If you have not changed your username, it should return something like this:

pi@raspberrypi ~ $

/home/pi

pi@raspberrypi ~ $

The cryptic command pwd shows the default directory you start at when you initialize the shell. As you notice, after returning the first request, the shell will immediately take you back to the command prompt, ready for the next command. Now enter this new command:

ls

The horizontal list returned is a list of directories and files inside the present working directory. The ls command essentially shows the list of folders in the folder you are working on.

To move through the directories, you will use the cd command, which means change directory. Try it with this command:

cd Desktop

You should notice that your command prompt changes to:

pi@raspberrypi ~/Desktop $

This is the same as opening the Desktop folder on a graphical user interface. When you enter the **ls** command, it will show you the list of files and folders inside the Desktop folder. Try it.

To confirm that you are within the Desktop directory, use the command **ls**.

Now, enter the command:

cd −

The command **cd −** takes you back to the previous directory, in our case, the **/home/pi** directory.

When you want to go back to the home directory, no matter what your present working directory is, you can always use the command **cd pi** where pi is your username. You can substitute pi with your username if you have changed it on your Raspberry Pi. Another way to get to the home directory is by using the **cd ~** command wherever you are in the file system. The ~ symbol is pronounced tilde and always points to the home directory.

Now, while on the home directory, enter this command:

cd desktop

You should encounter an error:

bash: cd: desktop: no such file or directory

What is the problem yet our desktop spelling is correct, and we know a directory with such spelling exists?

It is the capitalization. In the shell, '**Desktop**' is not the same as '**desktop**', just the way '**cd**' is not the same as '**Cd**' or '**CD**'. When working on the shell, you must be very specific about the commands and file and folder names.

One of the best things about commands is that you can tell the computer exactly what you want and it will behave exactly as you want it to. You can expand on commands using flags such as the – (minus) we used after **cd** – to return to the previous directory.

With time, you will learn that there are so many flags to use with almost every command. For instance, to list all the files and folders in your present working directory including hidden ones, you will use the **ls** command with the **–a** flag. Your command will look like this:

ls **–a**

If you use the above command on the home directory, the number of files and folders on your list should increase.

Now try **ls –l**. What do you see?

How about when you combine **–a** and **–l** in the **ls** command to have **ls –al**?

8.3 Summary

There are hundreds of Linux commands you will learn while getting familiar with and mastering the Shell. This is the most basic introduction meant for absolute beginners. There are countless resources on the internet that provide lists of common and even most useful commands you can print out and stick to your refrigerator or on your workspace.

Now that you know how the command line interface works, you should do a bit of practice before you move on to the next of hour of study where you will be introduced to real programming: Programming the Raspberry Pi using Python.

Hour 9: Programming the Raspberry Pi with Python

If you are an absolute beginner to the world of programming, you must have been marveled at how easily you could write a playable game using the simple Scratch tool that comes bundled with Raspbian OS on the Raspberry Pi.

Scratch is a great tool for learning the basics of programming, and especially visualizing how a practical program works. However, sooner or later, you are going to run into its limitations and that is when you are going to need a more powerful and versatile general purpose programming language. At this point, I introduce you to: Python.

9.1 What is Python?

You have already heard the term Python (in programming, not the snake or the Monty python) but if you do not know what it is, it is a high-level interpreted and dynamic language that features readable code.

The design philosophy of this popular and general purpose language focuses on beautiful and readable syntax, which makes it easy for programmers to express their concepts for a computer in fewer lines of code.

Unlike scratch, which is also easy to learn, Python is entirely text-based. This does not mean that you cannot use Python to create graphics; it basically means that the program code is purely text and not drag-and-drop blocks.

The Raspbian OS you installed on your Pi comes pre-loaded with a python development environment (known as IDE for integrated development environment) which allows you to input commands and create your program syntax with a helper. The integrated environment comes with the handy help() command that will provide answers to questions you may need answers to as well as a built-in text editor which is color-coded to guide along, as well as automated placement of indents.

Because Python is text-based, you can use any text editor to write and save your code; you are not limited to using the IDE although it helps. There are many text editors you can download and use, some, such as *Leafpad*, come pre-installed with the Raspbian. *Geany* is a popular choice for new Python programmers and Sublime Text is my personal favorite. Python files are saved with the extension .py.

You should however not use word processors with advanced formatting capabilities such as LibreOffice and Microsoft Word. These programs introduce special characters to the code during formatting that will prevent your programs running correctly.

9.2 Hello World! on Raspberry Pi

It has become an accepted tradition for every programmer's first program to be a hello world program—a simple program that displays the worlds "Hello World!" on the screen. Because we assume this is your first programming that is exactly where we are going to start.

On the desktop of your Raspberry Pi, you should see a Python logo shortcut to Python 3 IDE named IDLE 3. It looks like this:

Fig22: Python 3 IDE Shortcut

Start the Python 3 IDE by double-clicking this shortcut or by going to the Pi Menu then Programming and Python 3.

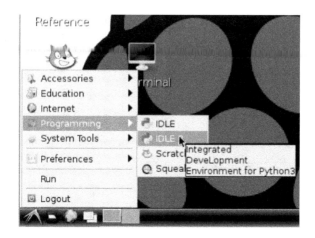

Fig 23: Starting the Python 3 IDE from the Pi Menu

Fig 24: IDLE 3program window

Raspbian, and all Linux distros, ship with Python 2 interpreter by default. However, it is recommended that you always use the Python 3 interpreter because they two are significantly different.

When you are on the Python 3 IDLE window, enter the following code on the first line then press enter:

>>>print ("Hello World!")

What this simple line of code does is tell the Python interpreter to print the phrase within the brackets and quotation marks on the computer screen. In this case, the phrase is Hello World.

Your line of code, however, is not saved in the computer memory, which is important when you want to create an actual program.

On the Python shell, click **File > New** to create a new blank text editor window to write and save your code.

On the new window, enter the hello world cord above. You will notice that the code is not run by the interpreter when you press enter. Save the code by clicking on **File > Save** or by pressing **Ctrl+S**. Give it the name **helloworld** and make sure that the file type selected is **Python Files** with extension **.py** or **pyw** before you click on the Save button.

9.3 Running a saved Python file

The best way for you to run a saved .py file is from the command line or the Terminal. Start the LXTerminal shell from the desktop. Ensure that your present working directory is the same one you saved the .py file. You can check using the command **pwd** and check the presence of the file using the command **dir**. In our case, the default directory is the same one we saved the helloworld.py file (/**home/pi/**).

Now enter the following command to run the file helloworld.py:

```
pi@respberrypi ~ $ python3 helloworld.py
```

An alternative approach is to first tell the system that the file you want to run is executable. You can do this using the command:

```
pi@respberrypi ~ $ chmod a+x helloworld.py
```

after declaring, you can then run the file using the command:

```
pi@respberrypi ~ $ ./helloworld.py
```

Note: Remember that names are case sensitive in the Terminal. Therefore, if you saved the file as "**helloworld.py**" and try to run "**Helloworld.py**", you will encounter an error.

If you run the program right, you should see the "Hello World!" text displayed on the screen. This shows that the program is running properly in the system, although at this point it is not a very useful program.

9.4 Learning to program Python

Python is a very simple to learn programming language but it is also very broad. We have created an in-depth 12 hour eBook that you can use to learn how to write programs that you can execute on your Raspberry Pi.

In this hour, we have covered what Python is and even created our first program to illustrate that you can create it on the Pi. However, we will not be covering the in-depth programming principles and how to create full-fledged programs in this book. We recommend that you check out our Python programming eBook 'Python: The No Nonsense Guide' if you are a beginner in programming for a complete guide.

9.5 Conclusion

The programs you will create for your Raspberry Pi using Python will be very practical in that you can use them to solve every day problems that you encounter. There are countless guides and ready-made tools and resources on the internet that you can use to simplify the process of designing and writing your own programs in Python. What is most important at this point is that you understand the process of creating and saving .py files and running them from the command line, all of which we have covered in this hour.

In the next hour, we will go in-depth to create a fully functioning Python app and run it on the Raspberry Pi. We suggest that you take some time between now and revert to Hour 10 and study as much as you can about programming in Python – the principles of correct syntax, importing libraries, and solving problems using simple code.

As a beginner in Python programming, and as a new owner of Raspberry Pi, it will not be long before you are a master in writing fully functional programs that make use of the hardware you have invested in. With a little practice and more studying, you will be able to program third-party hardware including sensors and output devices to make your Pi actually convert program code into action.

As a first step, we are going to dig deeper into Python on the Raspberry Pi and learn how we can make a LED light connected to a GPIO pin blink.

Hour 10: Writing More Code for Raspberry Pi in Python

We covered the introduction to Python in the previous hour and even went a step further to write out first program that writes text on the screen when run. You learnt how to run a .py file directly from the terminal using Python 3 and I mentioned that it was just the start. For this hour, we will cover more input and output of Python and write a simple code that can turn OFF and ON a LED light when certain conditions are met.

10.1 Input programming with Python

The input and output of a program are the most important for a budding programmer to learn, for the obvious reasons that the simplest functional programs must accept the user's input, process it, and give back a result.

While what we will create at this point may not be very useful, the most important thing you will learn is how to get the computer to do it. It is the principle and the method that matters. This will be starting point of the great things you will be able to program your Raspberry Pi to do – from building your own media center at home to developing an intelligent security system.

Start your Python IDLE from the desktop or by going to the **Pi Menu (Start) > Programming > IDLE 3**. We are going to write a simple program that will ask for the user's input then display the results.

First, we will learn about variables.

A variable is basically a reserved memory location that stores values. When you create a variable, you are asking the computer to reserve space in memory for a certain data type. The Python interpreter will allocate the memory such that the user input can be stored in.

We are going to create several variables for our new program. They are:

  name = A string variable to store the user's name

yearofbirth = An integer variable to store the user's year of birth.

city = A string variable to store the name of the city the user lives.

profession = A string variable to store the name of the user's profession.

On your blank script, enter the following code exactly as it appears:

name = input ("Enter your name: ")

yearofbirth = input ("What year were you born?: ")

city = input ("In which city do you live?: ")

profession = input ("What is the name of your profession?: ")

Save your code as *mydetails.py* or any other appropriate name you can think of, at a location you can easily access, preferably the default Pi directory on your Raspberry.

We are then going to run the code and see what it does. If you have forgotten how to run a .py file from the LXTerminal, go back to the last hour of this book to refresh your memory then try again.

If entered the code right, the program should prompt you to enter your name, the year you were born (in numbers), the city in which you live, and the name of your profession.

After you provide all this information, our program quits. This is because we have not programmed it to do anything further.

10.2 Adding comments to a Python script

There is no better point than this to introduce comments.

A comment in Python refers to something—text that is completely ignored by the Python interpreter. Comments are added to code as notes for yourself or other programmers who may want to understand what the code does. Comments are very important, as you will find out, and they are often preceded with the # (hash) symbol.

We are going to add comments to our code above to help us remember what the code does, and to tell someone looking at out code for the first time what it does. Modify your code to look like this:

#This program collects the user's details

name = input ("Enter your name: ")   #Prompt for user name

yearofbirth = input ("What year were you born?: ")#Prompt for year of birth

city = input ("In which city do you live?: ")   #Prompt for city

profession = input ("What is the name of your profession?: ")
            #Profession

When you save and run the above code, it will behave exactly as it did before you added comments.

10.3 Output programming in a Python script

Now that we have figured out how to make the Pi ask for information and the right way to leave comments on the code, we can go back to practicing making it output information.

We are going to add code that summarizes the name, age, city, and profession of the user. To achieve this, we will have to make a few modifications to the code like this:

#This program collects the user's details

name = input ("Enter your name: ")   #Prompt for user name

yearofbirth = int(input ("What year were you born?: "))   #Prompt   for year of birth and converts it to an integer.

city = input ("In which city do you live?: ")   #Prompt for city

profession = input ("What is the name of your profession?: ")   #Profession

age = 2017 - yearofbirth #Calculate age based on year of birth

print ("Hello. My name is", name, "and I am a", age, "year old", profession, "from", city +".")

What does your program output when you run the code?

10.4 Programming the GPIO with simple code

Since you are already familiar with connecting an electrical circuit to use with the Raspberry Pi, this step will be much simpler. You are going to learn to program the GPIO pins by configuring the GPIO library and light up a LED bulb when a certain condition is met.

As with the experiment we carried out in hour 7, we are going to use the power pin number 2 on the Raspberry Pi board to supply the power to the LED and you will connect the cathode (negative) leg of the bulb to any ground pin.

Now, modify your code to look like this:

#This program collects the user's details

import RPi.GPIO as GPIO #Command to import GPIO library

GPIO.setmode(GPIO.BOARD) #Set the board to use pin numbering

name = input ("Enter your name: ")   #Prompt for user name

yearofbirth = int(input ("What year were you born?: "))   #Prompt   for year of birth and converts it to an integer.

city = input ("In which city do you live?: ")   #Prompt for city

profession = input ("What is the name of your profession?: ")   #Profession

age = 2017 - yearofbirth #Calculate age based on year of birth

print ("Hello. My name is", name, "and I am a", age, "year old", profession, "from", city +".")

GPIO.setup(2, GPIO.OUT) #Setup GPIO Pin 2 to OUT

GPIO.output(2,True) #Turn GPIO pin 2 to ON

When you run the above code, you will need Super User priviledges. Start the LXTerminal and use the command:

```
sudo python3 mydetails.py
```

If your LED is connected to the right pin and there are no errors in the code, the LED should light up when the code prints the output.

Should you encounter *ImportError no module named rpi.gpio*, chances are you did not run the code with super user privileges or you may need to configure your GPIO library. You can learn more about this on https://pypi.python.org/pypi/RPi.GPIO.

10.5 Making the LED light blink

Making an LED light up with a simple Python code is no easy fete; you are on your way to doing wonderful things with your Raspberry Pi board. As a bonus for this hour, here is a simple code that you can use on your current script to make the LED blink rather than just light up.

Go through the code and try to understand what each line does then implement modifications of your own to make the light do all kinds of crazy things. Remember to add comments of your own as proof that you understand what the code does.

Good luck.

```python
import RPi.GPIO as GPIO #Import GPIO library
import time # Import the 'time' library to use 'sleep'

GPIO.setmode(GPIO.BOARD) #Use board pin numbering
GPIO.setup(2, GPIO.OUT) # Setup GPIO Pin 2 to OUT
#Define the Blink() function
def Blink(numTimes,speed):

    for i in range(0,numTimes):#Run loop numTimes

print "Iteration " + str(i+1)#Print current loop

GPIO.output(2,True)#Switch on pin 2

time.sleep(speed)#Wait time

GPIO.output(2,False)#Turn off pin 2

time.sleep(speed)#Wait

print "Complete" #When loop is complete, print "Complete"

GPIO.cleanup()

## Ask user for total number of blinks and length of each blink

iterations = int(input("Enter total number of times to blink: "))

speed = int(input("Enter length of each blink(seconds): "))

#Start Blink() function.

Blink (iterations), float(speed)
```

*Note: Indentations is very important. Observe it.

Hour 11: Reading and writing from GPIO ports from Python

Your decision to buy a Raspberry Pi was probably shaped by the knowledge that it is a board that has great extensibility—the capacity to connect many different external hardware to via the GPIO interface.

Even if you were not sure how much you could do with the Pi, by now, you probably already are planning a number of projects that could be classified as 'Physical Computing' because it involves programming third-party components and devices to be controlled by code written on the Pi.

In this 11th hour of the Raspberry Pi guide, we get to dive deeper into machine programming using the Python language and explore even further the powerful features of the Pi's GPIO pins majestically arranged on the top edge of your board. As you already know, these pins are the computer's interface to the outside world and at the simplest level, you can use them as input points you can connect sensors, and output points you can connect output devices.

11.1 Switching an LED on and off

In hour 10, we looked at how you can write Python code in a simple Python program we developed to turn on and off an LED bulb connected to the GPIO pins. We discovered that you need a Python library which provides a simple interface that you can use to manipulate everyday GPIO components. Luckily, because we installed the Raspbian OS, this library comes ready installed with the system.

But there is a simple way to manipulate an LED bulb without necessarily going around an existing code. This section of the book seeks to simplify how your Pi interfaces with both input and output hardware, and we will start with what we already know how to control – LED.

1. On your Raspberry Pi, start Python IDLE from the main menu. If you have forgotten, the process is Menu > Programming > Python3 (IDLE) or simply double click the shortcut icon on the desktop.
2. Start a new Python file and enter the following code:

```
import RPi.GPIO as GPIO

import time

GPIO.setmode(GPIO.BOARD)

GPIO.setup(2,GPIO.OUT)

GPIO.output(2,True)

Time.sleep(2)

GPIO.output(2,False)
```

3. Save your Python file and run it with administrator privileges (SUDO) to see what the code does.

An alternative approach to write a simple code that controls an LED bulb would look like this:

```
from gpiozero import LED

from time import sleep


led = LED(2)


while True:
```

```
led.on()

sleep(1)

led.off()

sleep(1)
```

With this Python code, you are choosing to use the BCM system of numbering the GPIO pins and not the BOARD system we used in the previous code. You can turn on the LED light using the code led.on() and turn it off using the code led.off(). For this example, the Python code will keep the LED bulb connected to Pin 2 flashing after every one second.

11.2 Connecting a push button to get input

As you can see from the example above, writing a simple code to control an output of electric current via a GPIO pin is pretty simple. But what would you need to do differently to program an input pin that controls a component, in our case a button?

For this demonstration, you are going to need:

1. Push button
2. Breadboard
3. female to male wire connectors.

Connecting a push button to your Raspberry Pi is as simple as connecting an LED bulb, except that we will use a different pin and a resistor is not necessary. In this case, we will use the listening port on Pin 3 (the second pin in the first row) and the other connection goes to any ground pin.

We will write a simple Python program that prints a short piece of text when the button is pressed.

Start your Python IDLE and create a new .py file with the following code:

```
from gpiozero import Button

button = Button(3)

button.wait_for_press()

print("Button Pressed!")
```

Save your code as a .py file, then connect the hardware as shown in the figure below:

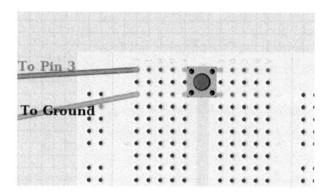

Fig :Connecting the push button to the Pins

Once your connection is in place, run the .py file from the Terminal with Superuser privileges. It should print text on the screen every time you push the button.

11.3 Controlling an LED bulb with a push button using Python

It will now be much easier for us to modify our program, and connect the LED bulb, such that when the button is pressed, the LED bulb lights up.

Modify your initial python program or open a new file from the IDLE platform and wnter the following code:

```
from gpiozero import LED, Button
```

```
from time import sleep


led = LED(2)

button = Button(3)


button.wait_for_press()

led.on()

sleep(1)

led.off()
```

If your connections are right, and you saved the code as it is, your LED bulb should light up for 1 second then turn off when you press the button on the breadboard.

Can you make modifications to the Python code to get three blinks of the LED bulb when the button is pressed?

11.4 Controlling the Brightness of an LED

So far, we have looked at how you can write a Python program that turns on and off an LED bulb. But how do you go about writing a code that can dim the light?

Raspberry Pi's RPI.GPIO library comes with a pulse-width modulation feature (popularly called PWM) that you can use to control the amount of power flowing from a pin to the LED, therefore controlling how bright it lights. In this example, you will connect the anode of the LED to pin 2 then run the code as a superuser.

```
import RPi.GPIO as GPIO

led = 2

GPIO.setmode(GPIO.BOARD)

GPIO.setup(led, GPIO.OUT)

pwm_led = GPIO.PWM(led, 500)

pwm_led.start(100)

while True:

        brightness = int (input ("Enter Brightness between 0 and
        100:"))

        pwm_led.ChangeDutyCycle(brightness)
```

Tip: Whenever you connect an LED to your Pi, make sure that you connect a resistor in parallel between it and the board. The resistor serves to limit the amount of current that flows through the LED to a safe level, to protect both the LED bulb and the GPIO pin that is the source of power.

Warning: When playing about with the GPIO pins, it is important that you exercise caution to keep your experiments safe and fun. Connecting devices and plugging wires randomly to pins on the board and especially power sources is a very risky thing to do and could completely brick your board and even cause fires.

Bad things can also happen if you connect devices and components that require a lot of power. It is safer to do your initial experiments using 5V LEDS because they pose less risk. However, do not graduate to connecting motors before you have a firm grip on what you are doing.

If you are unsure about a device or a component, or just want to protect yourself and your devices, you can consider getting an add-on board—they are available online for a few dollars. You can use such a board until a time when you are confident enough to use the GPIO directly.

11.5 Programming a button that toggles an LED on or off

Suppose you want to add a power switch that turns the LED on and off when pressed? Considering that we have already figured out how to make a button work as an input and how to connect an LED to a 5V power source, this section will focus only on the code.

```
from gpiozero import LED, Button

from time import sleep


led = LED(2)

button = Button(3)


while True:

        button.wait_for_press()

        led.toggle()
```

This code toggles the state of the LED between on and off in a loop. If you want to make the LED switch only when the button is pressed and held down, you can use two methods of the button class: when_pressed and when_released. Your code would look like this:

```
from gpiozero import LED, Button

from signal import pause
```

```
led = LED(2)

button = Button(3)


button.when_pressed = led.on

button.when_released = led.off


pause()
```

Save your code in a .py file and run it from the command prompt with superuser privileges to test it out.

Hour 12: How to Get the Most out of your Raspberry Pi

The moment you connect and fire up your Raspberry Pi 3, if it is your first time doing so, the journey to a world of programmable computers that can do almost anything with simple code will have begun. And believe us when we say it will never stop.

Just a few years ago, it was almost impossible for hobbyist programmers and DIYers to attempt machine programming, especially at such a low cost. However, we can agree that tiny computers such as the Pi have opened up a world where anyone with a little passion and $50 can automate almost every aspect of their life.

In this guide, we installed the Raspbian OS to the Pi, a distribution of Linux that has the benefit of being easy to master and laden with all the tools a beginner would need. However, with time, you may need to try out the many other types of operating systems that you can use on the Raspberry Pi including those specially designed for security systems, for IOT connected devices, and even home media centers.

There is a lot you can do to get the most out of your Raspberry Pi. In this section, we will highlight some of the basic projects and steps you should consider as you graduate out of the beginner's circle.

12.1 Try different operating systems

At the beginning of this book, we briefly touched on a few operating system options available for you to install on the Raspberry Pi 3. The list was in no way exhaustive. While NOOBS has demystified how an operating system is installed on the Pi, and Raspbian has been put together to bring all the tools you need to get started, it would be wise for you to begin sampling what other operating systems available have on offer and what their benefits are. Some of the most popular operating systems you should consider trying are:

1. Android (RTAndroid): This is a regularly updated version of Android designed for the Raspberry Pi. If you are an Android developer, or just wish you could take advantage of all the free software available on Google Play Store to make your Pi a fully functional computer, you should check out the video tutorial about this OS here: https://www.youtube.com/watch?v=cU7CEOmtmRk

2. Chromium OS: A group of passionate Rapberrians have come together to port Chromium OS to the Pi and other single board computers. So far, the group has released four editions of the ChromiumRPI. Note that this system is still in early developmental stages and should not be relied upon for everyday usage. You can check out what this OS is capable of on reddit here: https://www.reddit.com/r/chromiumRPI

3. Kali Linux: Are you a hacker or are looking for a dependable Linux distro for your security and penetration testing projects? If yes, then the ARM image of Kali Linux that runs smooth on the Pi may be what you are looking for. We have also written a complete eBook for beginners in hacking who may want to know how to get around Kali Linux tools called Hacking: The No Nonsense Guide. You can check out the eBook HERE. To see available images for your Raspberry Pi 3, go to https://www.offensive-security.com/kali-linux-arm-images/

4. OSMC: The Open Source Media Center os for Raspberry Pi is exactly what you guessed it is – a feature-rich media center software for home projects. This OS is based on Kodi, formerly known as XBMC. It is very easy to set up and use and easily passes as one of the best media center systems available for the Pi. It is also a great system to set up for non-techy people who just want a functional system that does not require too much tweaking. You can read more about OSMC on https://osmc.tv/.

5. Windows 10 IoT Core: If you are a windows fanatic, the Windows 10 version for the Raspberry Pi is exactly what you hope it is. This is not the full version of Windows 10, it is just a development platform that you can use to prototype your IoT projects and test connected devices. Still, it is very functional although only useful if you have another computer running windows 10 around. Discover more about this OS on Github http://ms-iot.github.io/content/en-US/Downloads.htm

12.2 Get a case with a built-in heat sink

Some Raspberry Pi owners believe that a case for the board and a heat sink is not necessary. For normal use and experiments, you would not need to cool the chip unless its temperature exceeds 100 degrees Celsius. However, if you overclock the Pi or need to use it on demanding tasks that keeps the SoC on full speed performance for long periods of time, we suggest that you get a heat sink to prevent possible damage of your Pi.

You can order a case with inbuilt sink or order them separately. The casing may be particularly important if you want to protect the board from the elements like water and dust or static charge introduced by fabrics and such. If you are going to buy a case for the Pi, consider getting an official one from the Raspberry Foundation to support the guys that bring us this magnificent $35 computer.

12.3 Explore a world of amazing learner projects

This book covers a tiny fraction of the things you can do with the Raspberry Pi. A simple search on the internet would show you the amazing myriad of projects that beginners such as yourself have managed to create over the years. The best way to get inspired to create something new is to check out what other Pi users have done with their boards, and often with a few third party components and circuits.

With a little investment and effort, you can easily add a camera module to your Pi, connect a touchscreen display, set up your own server, or even create your own cloud storage. In fact, if you are feeling ballsy, you can even buy a few sensors online and install a Raspberry Pi to autonomously drive your car!

The best part of this all is that you will be able to get support from the millions of users who share their code, tips, and tricks online on Reddit, social media, Stack Exchange, Github, and blogs. You can find some of the top places to seek inspiration in the section below.

BONUS #1: Raspberry Pi 3 Pinout Chart

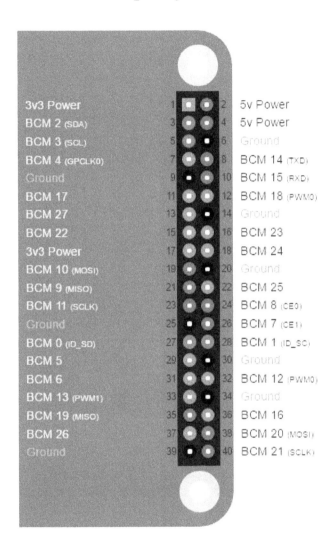

BONUS #2: The Top 6 Raspberry Pi Projects for Beginners

We all agree that Raspberry Pi, despite being credit-card sized, is a very dynamic microcontroller that has the capability to do just about anything you program it to do. It runs on the powerful Linux kernel and you can program it with plain Python language. There is no greater way to learn about coding and hardware hacking than through Raspberry Pi projects.

This is why we have put together a list of 6 of some of the best projects beginners like yourself have shared with the world. They should be inspiration enough to make you want to try them and even conceive better project ideas that you will share with the world.

1. DIY Raspberry Pi Music Player

In this project, you build your own music center using prebuilt software such as Pi's Musicbox and use a different device to control it such as your phone or remote controller.

Requirements

- Raspberry Pi
- 8 GB microSD Card

- Ethernet Cord or Wifi router
- Internet connection
- Mouse
- Keyboard
- USB drive

Link: https://pimylifeup.com/raspberry-pi-music-player/

Credit: Gus

2. Raspberry Pi Twitterbot

Wouldn't you like to make a bot that lives in your Raspberry Pi and interacts with the world via twitter? A builder on Instructables has done just this, in a project called Bot Collective to make Twitter bots that have physical Pi bodies and use the Twitter engine to communicate. You too can build one using the instructions made available.

Requirements:

- Raspberry Pi
- Mouse
- Keyboard
- Internet connection
- Second computer
- Smartphone

Link: http://www.instructables.com/id/Raspberry-Pi-Twitterbot/?ALLSTEPS

Credit: scottkildall

3. Raspberry Pi Personal Assistant.

Build a voice-controlled device using parts from an intercom system and a sound card. The guide on instructables will show you how to connect to the Pi via the intercom, install voice controller software, and add speech scripts that will return as audio outputs.

Requirements

- Raspberry pi.
- USB WiFi adapter
- USB soundcard
- Small 5V amplifier
- A 5V DPDT (Double Pole Double Throw) relays
- Some wires
- USB keyboard and mouse
- TV with HDMI or video in connection for installing everything on the Pi

Link: http://www.instructables.com/id/Raspberri-Personal-Assistant/

Credit: janw

4. Raspberry Pi Weather Station

Well, you could always check the five day weather forecast on TV or add a widget to the homescreen on your phone, but where is the fun in that when you can build a weather station of your own? This Raspberry Pi project does just that. You can accurately read temperature, wind speed, humidity, and atmospheric pressure among others with a simple build.

Requirements

- Raspberry Pi
- Pi camera
- Reed switches
- Sensors
- USB GPS chip
- Magnets
- MCP3008 chip
- Resistors
- Wireless adapter
- Waterproof case

Link: http://www.instructables.com/id/Complete-DIY-Raspberry-Pi-Weather-Station-with-Sof/?ALLSTEPS

5. Raspberry Pi Wall Mounted Google Calendar

The ultimate step of setting up a home personal assistant is how it communicates with you. One of the best implementations of a house assistant is by making a wall-mounted communication point, in this case, a digital calendar run by Raspberry Pi. This instructable will help guide you to understand general home networking and computing and how to bring the power of google into your tiny home computer.

Requirements

- Raspberry Pi
- Working home connection (Ethernet or Wi-Fi)
- Memory card
- AC Adapter
- USB wireless mouse and keyboard
- Wall mountable monitor with HDMI
- Wall bracket

Link: http://www.instructables.com/id/Raspberry-Pi-Wall-Mounted-Google-Calendar/

Credit: Piney

6. Raspberry Pi Personal Cloud Storage

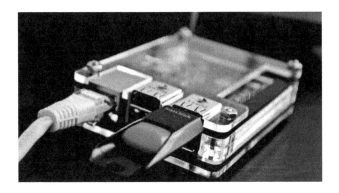

In this project, you can learn how to make your own cloud storage using Raspberry Pi. This is a computing system that will store your data on a local network to save you the bandwidth cost of constantly uploading and downloading data for local use. You will also be able to access your files from any connected computer over the internet.

Requirements

- Raspberry Pi
- Memory card
- Internet connection (Ethernet or Wi-Fi)
- External hard drive or USB drive
- USB keyboard and mouse
- Powered USB hub

Link: https://pimylifeup.com/raspberry-pi-owncloud/

Credit: Gus

So, which one of these projects are you going to start with?